Cantos *Poesia*

by David E. Matthews

Unlikely Books
www.UnlikelyStories.org
New Orleans, Louisiana

Cantos *Poesia*

Ten Dollars US

ISBN 978-0-9988925-8-0

First Printing

Unlikely Books
www.UnlikelyStories.org
New Orleans, Louisiana

for Fred Ramey
meine publick von einem

"Busy, busy, busy, is what we Bokononists whisper whenever we think of how complicated and unpredictable the machinery of life really is."

— Kurt Vonnegut Jr., *Cat's Cradle*

Intro - Metapoesia

What is poetry? I mean:
what is the meaning of poetry? I mean:
what is the definition of poetry?

This is *always* in the background of *all* we do . . .
as if poesia had a single mission statement, in a corporate sense
rather than 1000 in a randomly selected sample of 1000,
if you see how I mean . . .

Like, do you read the blurbs or the Preface of a book to decide whether or not?
These might describe the mission statement of the poesy inside,
But no two would ever be the same . . .
So now, temporarily,
we are discussing meta-meta-poetry
poetry about poetry about poetry:

One should speak plainly, one thinks
in poetry about poetry
rather than symbolically, metaphorically
about one's intentions,
so that one is understood,
as opposed to poetry
where it is not necessary to be understood

"the practice of metapoetry requires
the ability to reflect on the limitations of language
and develops genius."
Carnero and Paz -- Wikipedia/metapoesia

To speak in the common tongue
to speak of the commonplace
is the most basic of strategy to overcome
Man's Inability to Communicate (the limitations of language)
and the most commonplace in life, lore, & poesy is sex . . .

"A poet's function—do not be startled by this remark—is not to experience the poetic state: that is a private affair. His function is to create it in others. The poet is recognized—or at least everyone recognizes his own poet—by the simple fact that he causes his reader to become 'inspired.'"
Paul Valéry "Poetry and Abstract Thought"

Consider:

paradigm # 23974

inspiration	to thoughts of other-worldly heights
model	on the examples of ancestors, heros, & deities
influence	change opinions, mold perceptions
motivation	drive from point A to point B
impulse	liberate, unshackle
stimulation	arouse
catalyst	instigate
seduction	woo women

so the degree to which this, or any, poet overcomes his inability to communicate
due to the limitations of language
and succeeds in "inspiring" his auditor(s) to the effect he the poet seeks
might be the topic of our metapoesia

As to "developing genius"
we'll just have to agree-to-disagree:
no more than Ted Williams nor Tiger Woods could teach their individual genius
could any poet, or any school-of-thought, if you see what i mean . . .

"But if any man comes to the gates of poetry without the madness of the Muses, persuaded that skill alone will make him a good poet, then shall he and his works of sanity with him be brought to nought by the poetry of madness, and behold, their place is nowhere to be found."

Socrates (ca. 470-399 BCE) in the dialogue Phaedrus

We are not all genii
nor poets
and anyone who promotes himself has a fool for a reader

I know . . . I know . . . I know . . .

icanseeyadonwannatawkaboudit

"The move was genius, incredibly farsighted, far above any move that Deep Blue had played so far, so much so that Kasparov believed it must have been illegal ... Deep Blue had selected the move at random, something it was programmed to do in the event of a certain malfunction. But experts also believe that the move in question wasn't as brilliant as Kasparov thought it was either. Instead, it was weird and unexpected, which can be, in certain cases, even more devastating."

Andrew Blevins – via Paris Review

Nononononono

I don't think there's any difference between "weird & unexpected" and genius
I mean
familiarity with the classics
works of ordained genius
does not damp
the uniquity we assign to its space & time
but what that says about genius, creativity, and even ordinary intelligence . . .

icanseeyadonwannatawkaboudit

"all art is found art - but you have to be looking"

if you see how i mean, of course . . .
after years of intro-
speculation
& retro- I have arrived at the conclusion that "creativity"
is only a strategy to recognize & adopt
some anomaly in our perception of the normal/real world
and to the degree to which this anomaly is weird & unexpected is its genius
oh . . .

icanseeyadonwannatawkaboudit

but how else does one explain:

"the most glorious poetry that has ever been communicated to the world is probably a feeble shadow of the original conceptions of the poet."
Percy Bysshe Shelley

One has not to be Coleridge waked from a nap
to realize the crushing difference
between the dream and the realization –
that inability to communicate,
those limitations of language, again . . .
the artist conceives (and leave for now, just who or what is the inseminator)
gests in difficulty, births in agony & ecstasy, suffers in post-partum disappointment:
it is all some coefficient of talent & ambition . . .
dear, dear, dear –

icanseeyadonwannatawkaboudit

"Everybody's best work occurs in their head . . . the trick is to communicate it."

The Smith finds it by investing himself into what he pounds
The Midwife finds it by assisting the delivery
The Antenna finds it with openness to what is in the air

mis-communication & communication take the same bandwidth
one has one's opinion of how well one succeeds,
but the face of the auditor is another sign . . .
yes, yes, yes,

Icanseeyadonwannatawkaboudit

Between greed and fear lies moral certainty,
prevarications of the most believable sort,
that is, that is what everybody believes
the surety of those beliefs
is the gravity the poet seeks to escape,
but then they say
I heard what you said
I read what you wrote, but
I still don't know what you mean
So, lissen:

Idonwannatawkabouditanymoeither

song (poem)

Cantos Pasticcios

jīn golden

guāng light

huā flower

Ich denke dein

feast your eyes divine one on my yearning

long-longing unrequited

fidgetary cognitions

paradigm # 24057

if she wear no veil
if she covers not her hair
if she have short hair
if she shows some ankle
if she is unchaperoned
if she wear red high heels
if she wear no gloves
if she wear no girdle
if she is alone with a man not of her family
if she kisses on the first date

deep within the tumulting essence of myself,

of whom I sing

It's your thing,
do whacha wanna do.
I can't tell you
who to sock it to

or should it be "whom"?

encanto # 24202

i quake from desire
yet retreat unspoken
from fear my love lust
will be unwelcome

I care not, I dare care not,

for the rude

intrusion of your presence upon my happenstance

i repeal ringing
i reimage shining
i rescent sex
i relish feastiness
i retouch

Philopoesia

an inci-

dental

if not actually acci-

if she wear her skirt too short

jelly knees
cotton mouth
shaking hands

im-

posture *burning burning burning*

if she smokes
if she dances
if she drinks
if she drinks hard liquor

of ridiculable

ineptitude

if she lets a guy past 2nd base
if she has sex before marriage
if she has sex outside of marriage
if she has sex before 3rd date
if she has sex with strangers
if she dance naked
if she play in porn

in public in a premonstratively recriminality for disdemeanor writ

larg-

esse

ignobl-

oblige, if you see how I mean, that leaves only *kindersprechen*

inka dinka do, a dinka dee, a dinka doo

sedipoesia

Paradigm # 24206

high crime
felony
misdemeanor
moving violation
technical violation
violation
code violation
material sin
unethical act
transgression
indiscretion
inadvisable step
trespasses
infraction of the rules
not cricket
wrong!
bad manners
gaffe
misspoken
faux pas
misunderstanding
frankenprank
bad joke

trauma # 24209

every one is the hero of his own movie
every thing that he does is ok & groovy
every motive's clear as his conscience, he
need not scruple

but 'tis a two-edged-sword,
this complacency
for in this movie, for in this pageantry
events are scripted , with little latency:
duple tuple

ALL things that are, are

herein, in interactive reality
a step, a word, a choice, in practicality
must follow, *pro se*, in logicality -
no exceptions
surprise twists & endings,
deus ex machina
the Fates in matching polka-dot bikinae
unexpected events and things finikin
are exceptions
only insofar
as they are unexceptional

I plead with
the director of my movie
- myself -
for more clear direction,
but he demurs,
"I want your first reaction"
and he
air-quotes "inertia"

encanto # 24207

i become
i change
i am changed
i hate & fear
the Catalysm

i ripen
i age
i am aged
i hate & fear
the agent

my old self
who suffered so
matters not at all
to my new self
who is
become

we can not change

Lucidity Sun LI SOUTH FIRE FIRE Rebirth 離 Logos Fire CLINGING Yang South Circle Yang Sun Rebirth YANG REBIRTH Light Lucidity YANG Summer Light LIGHT CLINGING Li Yang Sun CLINGING Logos Logos FIRE REBIRTH Light Yang LIGHT CIRCLE Circle REBIRTH Logos Sun SOUTH LOGOS 離 Fire 離 Clinging SUMMER REBIRTH Circle LIGHT Fire 離 LOGOS YANG Sun South SUN South REBIRTH Li South REBIRTH LOGOS LUCIDITY Summer Fire SOUTH Summer CLINGING 離 Sun Summer Circle Sun CIRCLE CLINGING Light Yang LOGOS Rebirth South REBIRTH SUMMER Lucidity CLINGING LI SUMMER CLINGING CIRCLE CIRCLE Rebirth Summer YANG YANG Circle Summer Logos REBIRTH Sun Summer LOGOS SUN REBIRTH Lucidity Li Yang FIRE LUCIDITY Yang 離 REBIRTH Yang Clinging LIGHT Rebirth LI SUN LIGHT Summer SUN SUMMER Circle South LUCIDITY Lucidity Fire LIGHT Li LIGHT South SUN Circle LIGHT Lucidity SUN Clinging REBIRTH Light YANG Sun Lucidity FIRE YANG LOGOS SUN YANG Rebirth Light Fire LIGHT Circle

Incitapoesia

In dark
so complete
that an electric torch
just makes it seem darker
only proprioception
protects our shins & noses

a light
so piercing thru the dark
in pulses
intermittent,
strobe-meaning per morse code
so visceral it is
as if the clicking of the signal away
were your own
apoptosic switches
activated all-at-once
like downtown traffic lights
late, late at night

are you triggered?
so . . . fight or flight?

Tears for Fears
Shout
Shout
Let it all out
These are the
THINGS
I can do without

"it would be more convenient
for all men to carry about them
such things
as were necessary
to express
the particular business
they are to discourse on'
Those Laputans
with ... wealth ...
employed porters
to lug about
their vocabularies"
- ... Swift

paradigm # 24044

asceticism
austerity
teetotalism
abstinence
abstemiousness
temperance
sobriety
moderation
restraint
indulgence
excess
splurge
rabelaisian
bender
binge
profligacy
wretched excess
bacchanalian / dionysian / saturnalian
decadance
debauchery
orgy
hedonism

encanto # 24209

"Rouse ye, my people,
rouse ye! rouse ye! rouse ye!
Shake off the fatal stupor that is upon ye,
and hurl the usurping tyrant from his throne!
Impeach! Impeach! impeach! ...
Down with the dread boss monkey!
O, snake the seditious miscreant
out of the national ... tub
and reconstruct the Happy Family!"
– Twain, 1867

陳 Chen Thunder Arousing East Spring Yin Wood

l'eau de joie, comme l'eau de la vie, est une libation enivrante

out-of-nerve, and, out-of-my-
depth, yet, i assert
that the former is an *aperitif*; the latter, a *digestif*
liberations
of the mind, body, spirit
of the id, ego, superego
of the animal, anima, animus
of the conscience, conscious, unconscious
liberalisations
of all the sorts preacht so
vehemenously from sabbathian talking points
yet practiced so
assinuously on saturday night escapades
breaking-out
away-from-not-exactly-sure-what
hounded by premonstrations
deliberations merciless &
unjust,
if apprehended (is it not all known
before hand?)
yet, I assert that
the unshackled body is an uncontested verity (may we please agree on THAT?!)
the unshackled mind is totally allowed until it interferes with some-other-body
the unshackled spirit is totally allowed until it interferes with some-other-mind
if you see how I mean . . .
at the mall entrance to the department store
shy not away from the anxious young woman at the perfume counter with her
sample spritzer
she has *l'eau de la liberté*
on sale
individually or
in gift-packs of three, *avec joie et vie*
and you buy
for if some brands could make you sexy & mysterious
then why would this
brand not make you delirious (happy), lively & free?

stirb und
die and
werde
become

there

are

worse

things

than

death

(艮)
KEN
YANG
!

oracusations

your scowling approach, my
heart sinking
abruptly you say, "I have been
thinking"
I face the awful truth unblinking
stoicly

Sh
Sh-h-h-h
SH-H-H-H-H-H-H

M ota poesia

de librations de toxication

speechless in the *idea fora*
adjourned for lack of *quora*
warned to be on best *decora*
heroicly

SH-H-H-H-H-H-H

in flections in finity room

calmly recall sleepy-eyed trauma
reimagine phantasmagorma
launch out into intemperama
confutable

uncon trollable urgencies

follow the written-in-concrete script
pursue the jurious idee fict
the cyber imperative indict
immutable

SH-H

Paradigm
24225
Quiet
Hush of expectation
Calm before the storm
Peace of the
righteous
Tranquility
Still of
the night
Silence
of the grave

encanto # 24246
Walk with me.
Walk with me.
Please keep up

Matisse

"I do not paint that table, but the emotion it produces upon me."

"**Better**
to sleep
with
a sober **cannibal**
than
a drunk christian"
- Moby Dick

or for a Change

reason for

encanto # 21839

the difference,
he said
as he nodded
is whether
one is
the prodder
or
the prodded
- Mr. Lloyd

renaissance man
polymath
walking encyclopedia
fount of knowledge
mine of information
triple threat man
jack of all trades
utility player
generalist
factotum
handy man
critic
gadfly
know-it-all
sciolist
aficionado
amateur
dilettante

paradigm # 24110

oh, divine
Semele
meta fora
idea agora
mother of
Dion-
Where's-
The-
Party
?
he's
just
an excitable
boy
.
oh,
Cronos Demos
have you gotten
over-stimulated
again
?

these **things**
take time

No 'twas my grandson
I remain calm, Olympian
unfazed by terrestrial turmoil
.

does **any**body
really
know what
time it **is?**

you may as well dance
dance & drink, dance & drink
as contemplate
the caesarian abortion
polity has become

Potentiapoesia

these
things
I have
spoken
unto
you

babí léto

the English translation of this cesky is
"indian summer"
for it is the same time of year

indian summer – when nature is an indian giver
of nurturing warmth

the literal translation, however,
for babi leti is grandmother summer
and comes from the wisps of white webs
that float thru the air
this time of year -- I know not why

you won't see them in prague
well, maybe in the parks

in the parks you may see stará babička
selling flowers in desperate dignity
yea
with their thinning hair haplessly covert
with tattered pashmina

we took our flowers to Václavské náměstí
and laid them on the spot of Jan Palach

paradigm # 24020

encanto # 24272

if I god, was a
then myself, would do
but I mortal, canna
so I pray
to my will, bend the
world and this one person
to my desire, end the
delay
demos, use, news you can
an offer, refuse, she can
not resist downhill
momentum
fl"ing, she will pursue
dis-deigning, proffer
'jecting, will requite
testamentum

Mythopoesia

trauma # 24276

cronos demos perches on his precipice, with his drank, for the eveningly sundown ceremony and tonight's natural double-feature includes a blood, blue, super moon reflected over a still, small body of water

the looming lunar luminescence, lazer-like, indicts him, pointing from the far shore to the near and this is a sign, a providential, evidential proceeding in a court beyond our ken

- **judgement is final**

that light, thinks he,
shielding his eyes,
bounces off
the water at my feet
from the
blood, blue, super moon
filtered by
astronomical &
atmospheric conditions
shined by the sun

the sun fuses an eternity worth of fissionable material every nanosecond to make light & heat

we circle the sun and the moon circles us,
he muses, centerpunkt of
a very small system
a mere satellite
in the larger scheme of things

everything we see or seem is but a dream within a dream
-Poe

paradigm
 # 23998
amiri'? derivation
amiri'? allusion
amiri'? mention
amiri'? reference
amiri'? citation
amiri'? precis
amiri'? quotation
amiri'? excerpt
amiri'? Yūgen
amiri'? sampling
amiri'? borrowing
amiri'? lift
amiri'? appropriating
amiri'? arrogating
amiri'? plagiarization
amiri'? bootleg
amiri'? pirate
steal I'll say when

patapoesia

cronos demos takes one last look
before bed, to see the moon
now high, tiny, silver, seemingly solitary

- **perfectly round**

things I cannot explain

encanto # 24275
every action
has an
equal & opposite
inaction

LeRoi, boy, you're my friend
you say how and

Hettie? Genkai

poetry machine

as if

as if

chas. boyer
as
pepe le moko
leant
over
me
in
eluction
so complete
my
surrender
is given
"come
with
me
to
the
Casbah
where
we
shall
make
beautiful
poetry
togeth
er."

as if

ars poetica
took on
as many
meanings

as
we
could
imagine;
not only
poetic arts
but from the Latin
'to make art'
but also
that
arse
the
poet --
what
a
fool

one
could
say
'let
this
be
art
(or poetry)'

as if

the
urge
to
make
were
also
the
omnivolit
ion
and
the
omnip
oten
ce
nece
ssa
ry

proposition #1291 that the making must be equal parts certainty & uncertainty so that what is made is new & old, surprising & comforting, terrorfying & pleasing.

s y n o p o e s i a

imagine
a
world
not
created
but
rather
by
immaculate
proprioception
.
simply
came
into
being
beginning
with
the
first
two
motes
attracted
to
each
other
within
the
unified
field
of
interaction

and
so
it
went
on
until
the
scientific
inexorability
of
atomic
coagulation
emerged
into
what
we
now
call
the
realm
of
the
visible
from
which
point
it
was
also
inevitable
imperative

that
the
fusing
of
inanimate
matter
would
give
way
to
an
even
more
temporal
form
of
existence
until
the
point
where
the
survival
strategies
of
cellular
life
become
indistinguishable
from
the
normal

interactions
of
sentientities
.
the
fundamentals
of
these
evocumentaries
so
rudelementary
that
when
rediscovered
they
seem
mysterious
occult
profound
.
but tis just
permutation and
juxtaposition
of commonplace
verities each
of
which
individually
unremarkable
collectively astounding
.

Crisis

Sinology # 24169

JFK asserted in his inaugural address
that the chinese idiograms
for crisis & opportunity
were the same
but
haven't i read since then
that this synonymity is not correct?

i dunno

i thought that was why they cursed
'may you live in interesting times'

Opportunity

axiomoronic

this

disagreement is the mortar of society

. . .we are defined by our differences,
not our indifferences . . .1 . . .

friction

the

I know

discrepancy

this is contrary to conventional wisdom, which is wrong

understand
instead

that

when true

that it is like magnetic attraction

by which the opposite poles attract

it is said

and the apposite poles

tis the sum

repel

greater than its

oh --

climb down -- MOREover:

we live in a multi-polar world

parts

where attractions and

repulsions

when false

occur on a changing

the forest unseen

basis

for the trees

the foundation

of what we might call consensual reality

a framework

or the trees unseen

for understanding the world

for the forest

formed by communication with others, or rather,
by MIS-communication

abrades

for,

the

the more clear & precise
the more detailed the communication
the more likely to be understood
the more likely to be disagreed

individual

perception

till

if you see how I mean

it is some sort of cognitive dissonance

smooth enough to fit

the assigned

inherent in consciousness

that we

disguise our

cubby-hole

disagreements

• on the niggling / nitty-gritty details

or

comprehension

misapprehend the communication

in such a way that we agree with those with whom we disagree

of any sort

and disagree with those with whom we agree

may

at ear-popping platitudes

be

we are blind to the great sameness
as fish do not see water
as animals do not see air

ideal

but

only some disagreement reveals some shape

incomprehension

in the foggy cumuloplasm

is the norm

A self reference, viz. "IV9" from walk with me – sorry, not sorry

paradigm # 24287

moebius # 24288

fault

slip

slip-up

oversight

lapse

misstep

faux pas

goof

booboo

blooper

blunder

gaffe

error

mistake

miscalculation

howler

over-ambitious . . . over-optimistic . . . well-intentioned . . . naive . . . ultra-liberal . . . ultra-conservative . . . on the wrong side of history . . . set up with dumb-ass . . . wrong as the day is long . . . poorly reasoned . . . based on discredited assertions . . . ignorant of certain salient facts . . . uninformed . . . working from flawed assumptions . . . poorly executed . . . ill-conceived & wrong-headed . . . sadly mistaken . . . smokin' the silly weed . . . starry-eyed . . . daydreamer . . . unrealistic . . .

mis-steps
mark
our
progress
more than
intent
.
in evolution
this is called
mutation
;
in law
this is called
legislation
;
in politics
the current avatar is
trump
;
in competition,
upset
;
in literature,
poesia
.
indeed
all of life
is a happy accident
but you wouldn't know it
to hear
some people
if you know what i mean
.

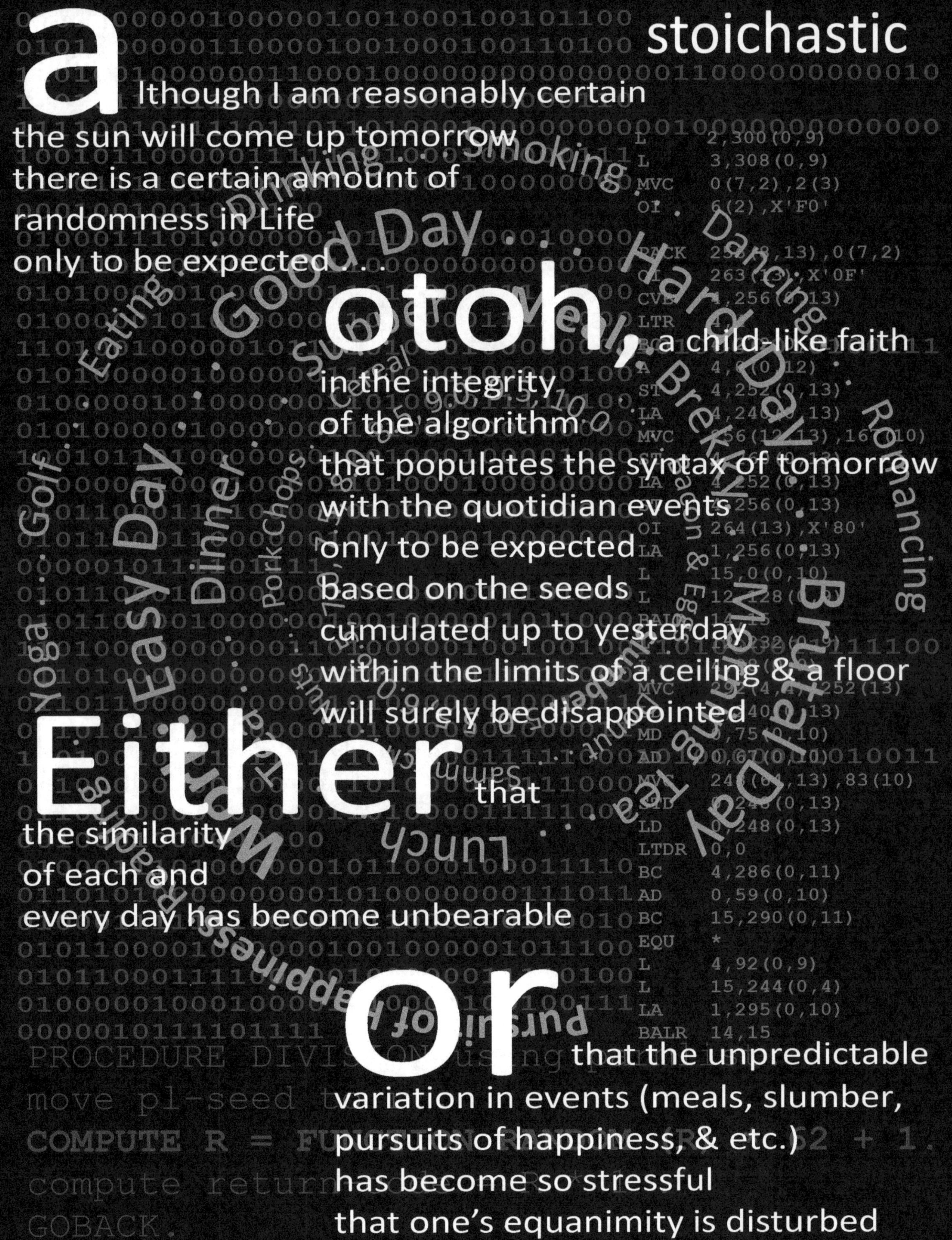
stoichastic
although I am reasonably certain
the sun will come up tomorrow
there is a certain amount of
randomness in Life
only to be expected . . .
otoh, a child-like faith
in the integrity
of the algorithm
that populates the syntax of tomorrow
with the quotidian events
only to be expected
based on the seeds
cumulated up to yesterday
within the limits of a ceiling & a floor
will surely be disappointed
Either that
the similarity
of each and
every day has become unbearable
or that the unpredictable
variation in events (meals, slumber,
pursuits of happiness, & etc.)
has become so stressful
that one's equanimity is disturbed

Sympoesia

silly me your
indifferent smile
and smug silence
sez
you think me dense
tho' I think I danse
you think me dunce

intoxication were
introduced
by romans
to numbify
opponents with
poisoned arrow

p-i-i-l-n-n-n-n-n-g-g-g

sniff
smell
wet your whistle
taste
sample
nip
sip
take a drop
cut the dust
cut the trench
imbibe
drink
tipple
swig
slug
have a couple of pops
throw back
knock back
toss down
slurp
gulp
quaff
lap up
hit the bottle
guzzle
swill
glug down
pop a few corks
chugalug
overindulge
drown your sorrows
binge
tie one on
paint the town red
spree
go on a lost weekend
go on a bender

p-i-i-l-n-n-n-n-n-g-g-g

it's not that I am old
you explain with a sigh
tho' my stance is
stoop'ed
and my pate is bald
'tis that me & my
anacreonies
russet too many
acrimonies
in the guise of
mien ancien

p-i-i-l-n-n-n-n-n-g-g-g

now we
peace-loving fellows
auto-intoxicate

p-i-i-l-n-n-n-n-n-g-g-g

as per Dr. Jonson
are we not the
most human
on display
we beasts, those –
with the
most to
forget

I thought I was
put out to stud
but 'twas only to
pasture

p-i-i-l-n-n-n-n-n-g-g-g

paradigm # 24309

p-i-i-l-n-n-n-n-n-g-g-g

Anacreonism

Zuò

trauma # 24214

a woman at the mall
interesting looking, rather than ravishing
partially obscured by her flannel shirt
her t-shirt
"Don't look back. You're not going that way"
sez
interesting thought, rather than brilliant
to defend Satchel Paige
the traffic cop stop straight-arm
never done this before –
but, a pic of your shirt, please
and she agrees
oh-h-h-h-h
pull back your flannel shirt
with your thumbs
hands on your hips
so I can see the slogan
<snap>
u-h-h-h-h-h
point forward
tuck your chin like a fighter
<snap>
a-h-h-h-h-h
one foot forward
and gimme more bulldog
<snap>
hah!
more athletic
<snap>
hah!
head back, chest out
hand up like you're holding a sword
<snap>
that's good
email you a copy

encanto # 24281

she walks in beauty
thru the fluoro-lit corridors of commerce
glowing like a green plant in the desert
nourished by deep roots
confidentially strident
among the grey-people I do not see
– some serious side-eye
so placidly does she proceed
amid the noise & haste
herself, intent, engaged,
amicable, approachable
that I am emboldened,
when normally I am shy
– I beg your pardon
her wide-eye surprise,
possibly feignt, is so endearing
I am struck dumb,
speechless & stuttering
but in broken phrases
I circumspect my interest
– sexual availability
today, this hour,
maybe nothing will come of it
but I've already touched her infinite

paradigm # 24226

Please excuse me
Could we talk later?
I can't talk to you
I think you've had too much to drink.
I don't want to talk to you now
Scram, weirdo!
Buzz off, creep!
Beat it, loser!
Drop dead, dodo!
Take your hands off me!
Let me go!
I'm out of here!
Help!
Help, police!

being or being not? been or been not? have or have not? has or has not? had or had not? do or do not? did or did not? am or am not? will or will not? shall or shall not? should or should not? would or would not? could or could not? can or cannot? must or must not? might or might not? may or may not?

shì

koan # 24119

so i asked my yoga teacher what time was it
and she said: Now—
and i said very funny yogi
you can tell me what time it will be in an hour, instead
and i'll work it out . . .
it IS Now, she said

retrocausality

The things we will do in the future
Affect the present
Affect the past

It is all there to see right in front of us
In our present
In our past

Even not a gypsy may tell your future
By your present
By your past

Of course,

Even not a gypsy *only* may tell your future
But
The uncertainty of may / may not
Means it all means *no*thing

Yet
It *does* seem like *some*thing, in hindsight
But people *do* change *some*times
And so, *some*times, we are surprised
Even then
Looking back, *some* will say
I *knew* it, I just didn't *know I knew* it . . .

<table>
<tr><td>Eco, grafioso
Trains for
Tenaha, Timpson, Bobo & Blair –
Naaaaa-cog-DOCHes –
LUF-kin –
DI-bol WAKE-field –
CORR-igan
MOS-COW –
7 Oaks LEGG-ett –
LIV-ingston –
COLDspring SHEPhard –
Cleveland SPLEN-DORa –
HUM-ble –
A-n-n-n-n-n-n-d Hou-STON . . .</td><td>Rapido, sotto
||:
Wobble, Bobble, Turnover & Stop
: ||~4

||:
Wobble, Bobble, Turnover & Stop
: ||~n</td><td></td></tr>
<tr><td></td><td></td><td></td></tr>
<tr><td>Now leaving on Track Two . . .BOARD!</td><td>Kachooo – Kachank – Kachunk!</td><td></td></tr>
<tr><td>Hooo-hooooo-hoo</td><td>Hooo-hooooo-hoo</td><td>Dissonata, lamentoso</td></tr>
<tr><td>Shooosh, squeal, chuffa-chuffa-chuffa</td><td>Shooosh, squeal, chuffa-chuffa-chuffa</td><td><Accelerare e crescere ogni iterazione></td></tr>
<tr><td>1)
This train be for believers, be leavin' here today.
I'm gonna be on that train no matter what they say.</td><td>clickety-clack, clickety-clack, clickety-clickety-clickety-clack
clickety-clack, clickety-clack, clickety-clickety-clickety-clack</td><td></td></tr>
<tr><td>clickety-clack, clickety-clack, clickety-clickety-clickety-clack
clickety-clack, clickety-clack, clickety-clickety-clickety-clack</td><td>May be bound for heaven, may be bound for Hell.
May be bound for nowhere, baby -- nobody can tell.</td><td></td></tr>
<tr><td>woo-hoooooooooooooooooooo-hoo-hoo-hoo!</td><td>woo-hoooooooooooooooooooo-hoo-hoo-hoo</td><td>Dissonata, come Dylan</td></tr>
<tr><td></td><td></td><td></td></tr>
<tr><td>Chorus:
Clickety-clack, clickety-clack, clickety-clickety-clickety-clack –</td><td>Clickety-clack, clickety-clack, clickety-clickety-clickety-clack –</td><td></td></tr>
<tr><td>"How we doin', Fred?"</td><td>Clickety-clack, clickety-clack, clickety-clickety-clickety-clack –</td><td></td></tr>
<tr><td>Clickety-clack, clickety-clack, clickety-clickety-clickety-clack –</td><td>"Little Late, Charley"</td><td></td></tr>
<tr><td>"Last call for the diner!"</td><td>Clickety-clack, clickety-clack, clickety-clickety-clickety-clack –</td><td></td></tr>
<tr><td>Woo-HOOOOOoooooooooooooooooooo</td><td>Woo-HOOOOOoooooooooooooooooooo</td><td>Dissonata, Doppler-Shift</td></tr>
</table>

Clickety-clack, clickety-clack, clickety-clickety-clickety-clack –	"Tickets, tickets, tickets."	
"Peanuts, soda pop, popcorn, candy!"	Clickety-clack, clickety-clack, clickety-clickety-clickety-clack –	
Clickety-clack, clickety-clack, clickety-clickety-clickety-clack –	"Last call for the diner!"	
Clickety-clack, clickety-clack, clickety-clickety-clickety-clack	Clickety-clack, clickety-clack, clickety-clickety-clickety-clack	
Whoo-HOOooo, WHOO-HOOooo, WooHOOooo	Whoo-HOOooo, WHOO-HOOooo, WooHOOooo	*Dissonata, Urgento*
2) Red light ahead is blinkin', don' know what it means. This train of thought I'm thinkin' is full of tragic scenes.	clickety-clack, clickety-clack, clickety-clickety-clickety-clack ding-daing-dang, ding-daing-dang, ding-daing-dang, ding-daing-dang	*Dissonata, dopller-shift*
clickety-clack, clickety-clack, clickety-clickety-clickety-clack clickety-clack, clickety-clack, clickety-clickety-clickety-clack	There's death & lies & compromise & broken-heart-ache, too, No matter what the sighs of freight, this train keeps pullin through.	
woo-hoooooooooooooooooo - how 'bout you?	woo-hoooooooooooooooooo - how 'bout you?	*Dissonata, come Dylan*
Chorus:		
3)		
Roarin' down Dead Man's Leap I can't slow down tho' it's steep	clickety-clack, clickety-clack, clickety-clickety-clickety-clack clickety-clack, clickety-clack, clickety-clickety-clickety-clack	
clickety-clack, clickety-clack, clickety-clickety-clickety-clack clickety-clack, clickety-clack, clickety-clickety-clickety-clack	I've gotta schedule to keep And miles to go before I sleep	
	Before I sleep, before I sleep Miles to go before I sleep Before I sleep, before I sleep Miles to go before I sleep	*Rapido, decrescendo*
Chorus:		
4)		
Somethin' on the tracks ahead I caint see in this light clickety-clack, clickety-clack, clickety-clickety-clickety-clack clickety-clack, clickety-clack, clickety-clickety-clickety-clack	clickety-clack, clickety-clack, clickety-clickety-clickety-clack clickety-clack, clickety-clack, clickety-clickety-clickety-clack I'm feelin some awful dread Something idn't right	
The tracks is loose, we're off the rails *Sssssssssss-boom- bah!* *Whizzzzzzzzz- crash-boom-squeal-scream* *Scraping-slamming-grinding-steam*	*OHHHHHH!!! AGGGGGHHH!!! EEEE!!!* 's all she wrote, dead as doornails *Whizzzzzzzzz- crash-boom-squeal-scream* *Scraping-slamming-grinding-steam*	*Dissonata, disgiunto*

duetto
they met at a midnight crossing
but they'll never meet again
for one was an east-bound freight
and the other, a west-bound passenger train

Dissonata, lamentoso
Heooooo-ooooooooo

Con finalita
Shush-sh-sh-sh

V	*Pitch/Vol./Speed/mode*	I.	
S:		0	
A:	*Humilis/Sotto/largo/etheriale*	4	Make me / an instrument / of His peace
T:	*Altis/sotto/largo/etheriale*	4	Make me / an instrument / of His peace
B:		0	

V	*Pitch/Vol./Speed/mode*	I.	
S:	*Altis/sussurro udibile /rapido/sprezzatola*	8	Make me an instrument --
A:		0	
T:		0	
B:	*Gutturale/murmurare/regulare/sprezzatola*	8	-- of His peace

V	*Pitch/Vol./Speed/mode*	I.	
S:		0	
A:	*Reg./sotto/molto largo/ephemerale*	2	Make me (2) an instrument of His peace
T:	*Altis/reg./largo/stentor.*	4	Make me (2) an instrument of His peace
B:	*utturale/murmurare/regulare/sprezzatola*	8	Make me an instrument of His peace

V	*Pitch/Vol./Speed/mode*	I.	
S:	*Reg./sotto/reg./imposito*	8	Make me an instrument of His peace
A:	*Reg./sotto/molto largo/ephemerale*	4	Make me (2) an instrument of His peace
T:	*Altis/reg./largo/preghiera*	2	Make me (2) an instrument of His peace
B:	*gutturale/murmurare/molto largo/funda.*	1	Make me an instrument of His peace

rondo

V	*Pitch/Vol./Speed/mode*	I.	
S:	*Reg./reg/reg./imposito*	4	Make me (2) an instrument of His peace
A:	*Reg./reg/reg./ephemerale*	4	Make me (2) an instrument of His peace
T:	*Reg./reg./reg./preghiera*	4	Make me (2) an instrument of His peace
B:	*Reg./reg./molto largo/funda.*	4	Make me an instrument of His peace

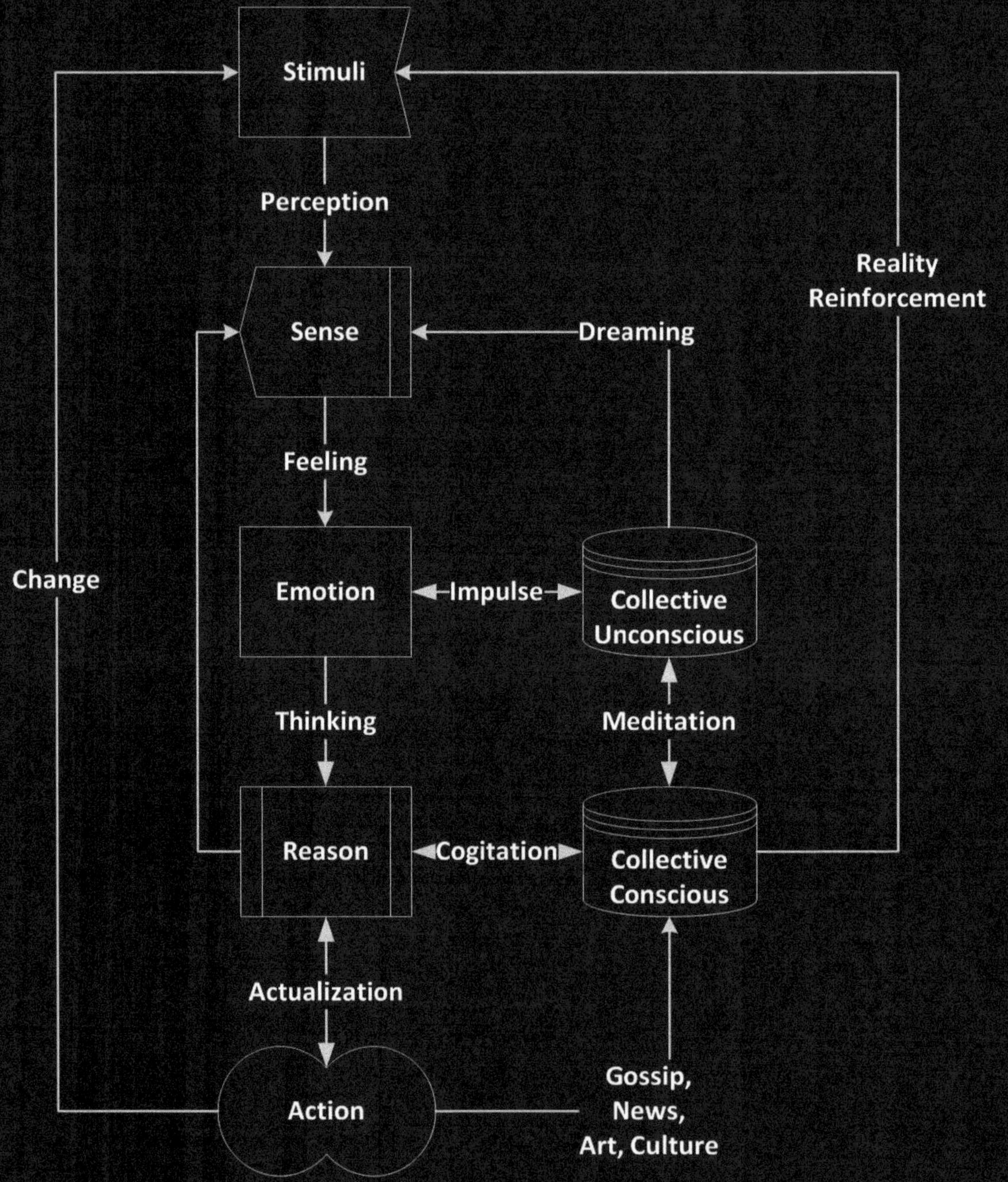
Feedback Loop of Collective Reality
Stimuli
Perception
Sense
Dreaming
Reality
Reinforcement
Feeling
Change
Emotion
Impulse
Collective
Unconscious
Thinking
Meditation
Reason
Cogitation
Collective
Conscious
Actualization
Action
Gossip,
News,
Art, Culture

Editor's Notes

When one first sits down to the meat of **Cantos *Poesia***, one is inclined to take each individual page as a single work of art. The layered pages and shifting text invite such an approach, and the reader is rewarded by it, as each page unfolds into a asymmetrical experience of beauty.

By now, you might've noticed that the book wasn't actually designed that way. Pages 7-10 constitute the obvious example: they are a single poem called "Metapoesia," spanning four pages of skewed iconography with a straightforward textual message. A closer look at page 29 reveals it is three discrete poems: "trauma # 24214," "paradigm # 24226," and "encanto # 24281," interwoven into what can then be described as a single visual poem, a single work of art.

When David E. Matthews first sent this manuscript to me, then called ***and* in *other* things, *also*** (an excellent title, but one that would be impossible to Google, especially given the author's common name), he included a table of contents or the beginning of the book, detailing the elements of each page; the original poems as he wrote them, before visual recombination. I found that the table, while enlightening, distracted from my initial enjoyment of the book. I found that it was interesting to explore David's intent upon my third or fourth reading, but when I first sat down to these extraordinary pages, I wanted to experience each one individually, without digging for structural clues. I opined that the table of contents go in the back of the book, as Appendix A, and that David should write a short afterword explaining a bit about his process. David replied that he didn't care if the afterword was short or long, so long as he didn't have to write it.

Cantos *Poesia*, as the Vonnegut epigraph alludes, is about the machinery of the universe. It draws its perception thereof from the I Ching and *The Secret of the Golden Flower*. This is most clearly illustrated in the *Cantos Pasticcios* (pages 11-19). The *Cantos Pasticcios* are the heart of **Cantos *Poesia***, assembling not only an exciting variety of textual and visual elements, but the author's core metaphysic, built on the aforementioned occult sources and brought into a contemporary framework. The *Cantos Pasticcios* are further described by Appendices B and C, which reveal each page's connection to the basic eight trigrams of the I Ching. Appendix D is a glossary of Czech terms; David lived in the Czech Republic from 2009 to 2014, and explores the interplay between Czech, German, and English throughout the book.

The publisher of this volume, Unlikely Books (which I run as an independent micropress), is the daughter company of an electronic magazine, *Unlikely Stories*, which has been running more-or-less continuously since 1998. Several of the **Cantos** have been published in that journal. David has previously written seven books of poetry, all self-published and available through Amazon. A list of David's books, as well as other Unlikely Books, follow the appendices.

—Jonathan Penton

Appendix A
Contents

Appendix B

#	SubTitle	Trigram	mneme	Meaning	paradigm	thing	quote	FBLoop	front	encanto	Y/Y
1	Philopoesia	Eros/kan	seduction	woo women	24057 If she	Its your thing	Inka dinka	waking pleasure	Non-seq Feast your eyes divine	#24202 I quake from desire	yin
2	Sedipoesia	Rebirth/li	catalyst	instigate	24206 Wrong!	Things we cannot change	All things that are, are light.	Traum	Sapphic #24209 finikin	#24207 catalysm	yang
3	Incitapoesia	Arousing/ chen	stimulation	arouse	24044 Asceticism-hedonism	Things I can do without	Swift laputans	stimuli	Non-seq In dark	#24209 presentim ent	yin
4	Impetapoesia	Joy / tui	impulse	liberate, unshackle	24219 joy	My favorite things	Duchamp ideas	sense	Non-seq Eau de joie	#24220 Freud-duh!	yin
5	Motapoesia-	Stirb und werde / ken	motivation	drive from point A to point B	24225 silence	things worse than death	Matisse not the thing, emotion	emotion	Sapphic oracusati ons	#24246 Walk with me	yang
6	Potentiapoesia-	Receptive / kun	influence	change opinions, mold perceptions	24110 Gadfly-Renaissance man	These things take time	Drunk cannibal	reason	semele	#21839 goad	yin
7	Mythopoesia-	Heaven/ chien	model	on the examples of ancestors, heroes, & deities	24020 Thing-actual-ization	things I have spoken to you	The play is the thing.	action	Babi leto	#24272 unwilling	yang
8	Patapoesia	Ideation/ sun	inspiration	to thoughts of other-worldly heights	23998 Deriving-steal	Things I can't explain	dream within dream	change	trauma #24276	#24275 every action	yang

Appendix C

K'an the Abysmal, water,
the moon
N
Ch'ien, the Creative,
heaven
Ken, Keeping Still,
the mountain, stillness
Tui, the Joyous,
lake, mist
W
Chen, the Arousing,
wood, thunder
E
K'un, the Receptive,
earth
Sun, the Gentle, wind,
the penetrating
S
Li, the Clinging,
fire, light, sun,
warmth

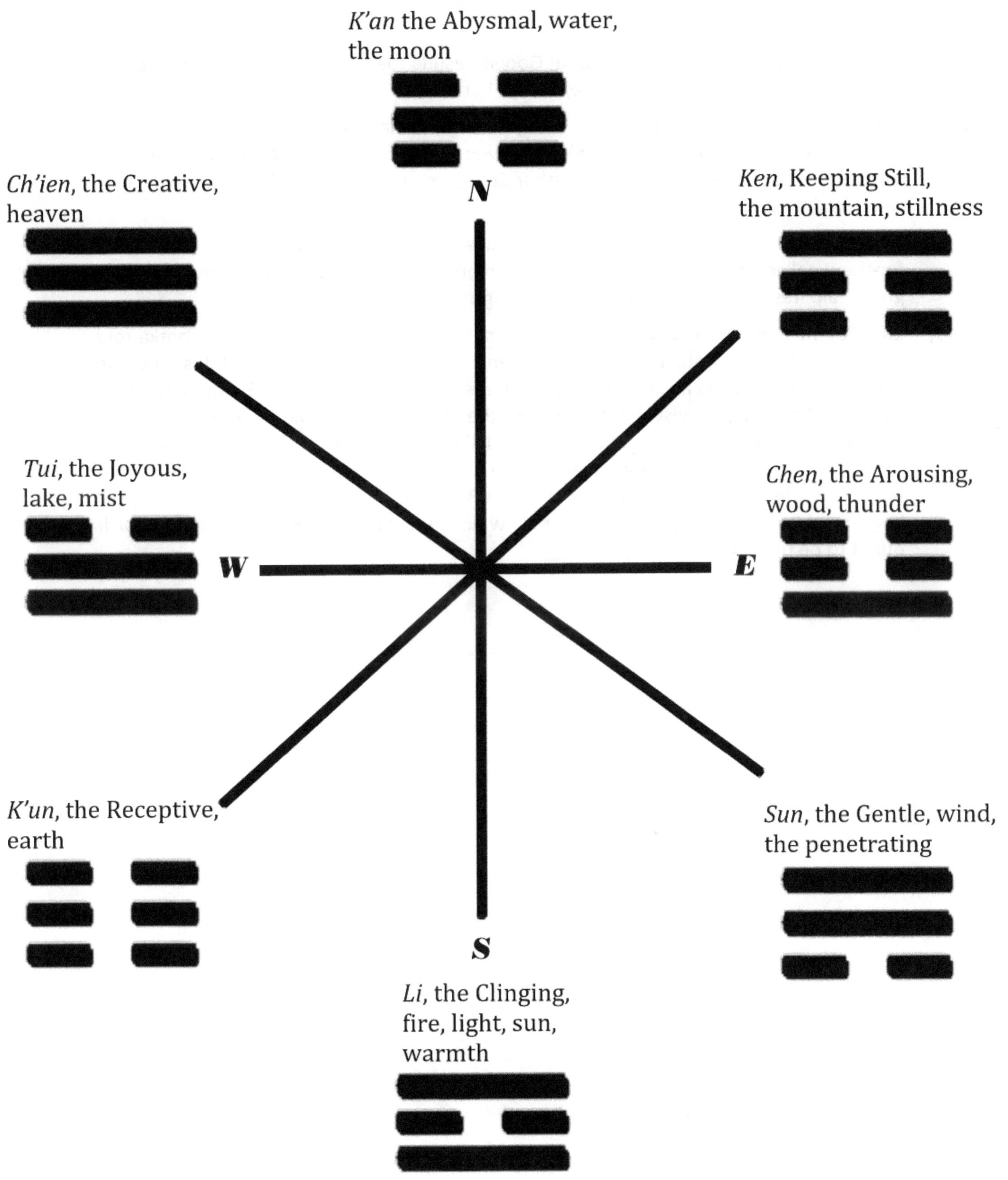

Appendix D
Czech Glossary

hoedown from Cesky 'hody,' meaning feast. In Google results the synonyms given include party, shindig, hootenanny, bash, jamboree, dance, barn dance, baile, fête, celebration.

barn from barley arn (barley house) from Cesky suffix meaning house '-arna,' as in kavarna (coffeehouse), vinarna (wine house), and even a sign we saw in Vyton, bramborarna (potato house). James McWhorter, author & linguist, wrote he didn't know where -arn came from BUT I DO!

a tisket, a tasket from Cesky 'tesky tasky' meaning heavy bag. As mrs came in thru the closed-for-the-weekend entrance to our apartment in prague with two big bags of groceries, the guard said 'tesky tasky' and pointed to the bags.

ahoy from 'ajoj' meaning hello, goodbye, and cheers, like aloha. My physician Dr. Sobotka told me it came from the Latin phrase *ad honorem jesu*, in honor of Jesus, AHoJ. Just because in English this is mainly a nautical term of address of long duration (1745) and that CZ is a landlocked country, linguists have disdained the idea that this could be an Anglicisation, but I will not yield. I will not give up. Eventually the weight of the list of all the Cesky Anglicizations I find will change minds. I just finished reading *Old Prague Tales* by Jan Neruda, published in 1873. In a story called "A Beggar Brought To Ruin" when she trys to beg, she starts "Praised Be The Lord Jesus" which I would love to see the original, cuz it **ought** to be translated as "Ahoj".

Other Titles by David E. Matthews

My S-Word: 1972-1999 (published 2017)

Better Late Than Never—Sez Who? (written 2000-02, published 2017)

Back to Confucius (written 2002-05, published 2015)

walk with me (written 2005-10, published 2015)

beyond: (written 2010-11, published 2016)

v1 (written 2010-11, published 2017)

Traum von dem Gescheitert Dichter: (the dreams of a failed poet) (written 2015-18, published 2018)

Other Titles from Unlikely Books

Left Hand Dharma: New and Selected Poems by Belinda Subraman

Apocalyptics by C. Derick Varn

Pachuco Skull with Sombrero, Los Angeles 1970 by Lawrence Welsh

Monolith by Anne McMillen (Second Edition)

When Red Blood Cells Leak by Anne McMillen (Second Edition)

My Hands Were Clean by Tom Bradley (Second Edition)

anonymous gun. by Kurtice Kucheman (Second Edition)

Soy solo palabras but wish to be a city by Leon De la Rósa and Gui.ra.ga7 (Second Edition)

Blue Rooms, Black Holes, White Lights by Belinda Subraman (Second Edition)

Scorpions by Joel Chace

Ghazals 1-59 and Other Poems by Sheila E. Murphy and Michelle Greenblatt

brain : storm by Michelle Greenblatt (Second Edition, originally anabasis Press)

My Hands Were Clean by Tom Bradley (Second Edition)

Definitions of Obscurity by Vernon Frazer and Michelle Greenblatt (Second Edition of *Dark Hope*, Argotist E-Books)

ANCHOR WHAT by Vernon Frazer

ASHES AND SEEDS by Michelle Greenblatt

Love and Other Lethal Things by K. R. Copeland

_a ship on the line by Vincent A. Cellucci and Christopher Shipman

#specialcharacters by Larissa Shmailo

Beautiful Rush by Marc Vincenz

We'll See Who Seduces Whom by Tom Bradley

pleth by j/j hastain and Marthe Reed

Gods of a Ransacked Century by Marc Vincenz

www.ingramcontent.com/pod-product-compliance
Lightning Source LLC
LaVergne TN
LVHW081425110826
845149LV00010B/1867

* 9 7 8 0 9 9 8 8 9 2 5 8 0 *